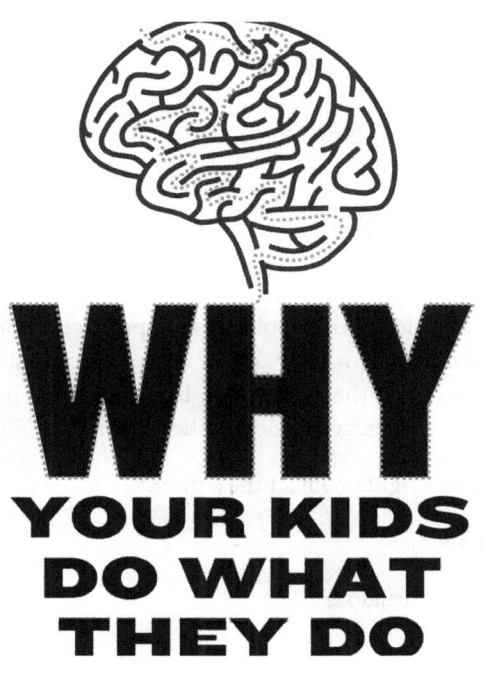

WHY
YOUR KIDS DO WHAT THEY DO

WORKBOOK

Copyright © 2023 by Rodney Gage

Published by Four Rivers Media

All rights reserved. No portion of this book may be reproduced, stored in a retrieval system, or transmitted in any form or by any means—electronic, mechanical, photocopy, recording, scanning, or other—except for brief quotations in critical reviews or articles, without prior written permission of the author.

For foreign and subsidiary rights, contact the author.

Cover design by Sara Young

Cover photo by Gabriela Furtado

ISBN: 978-1-959095-16-3   1 2 3 4 5 6 7 8 9 10

Printed in the United States of America

RODNEY GAGE

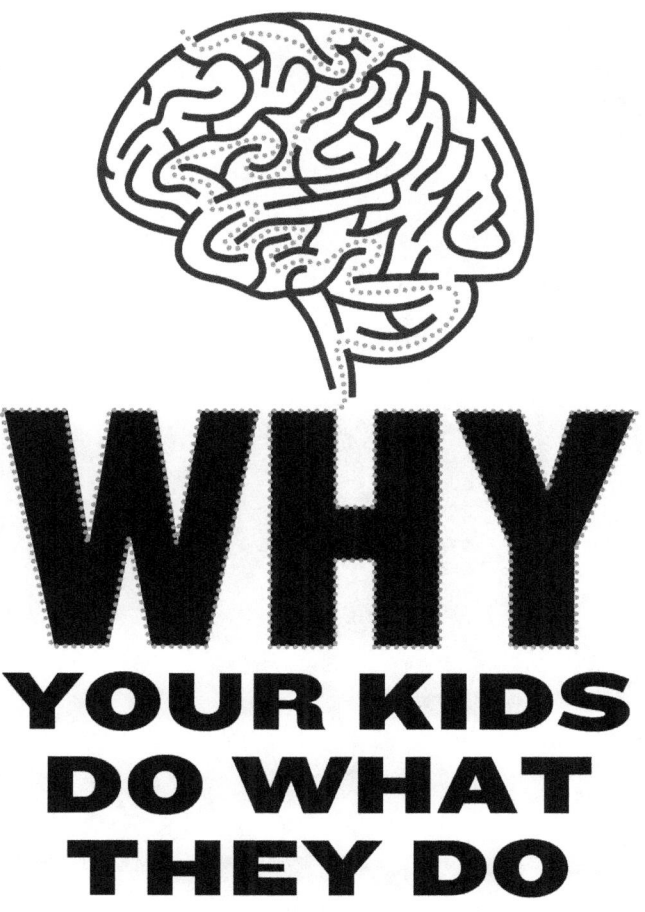

WHY
YOUR KIDS DO WHAT THEY DO

RESPONDING TO THE DRIVING FORCES BEHIND YOUR TEEN'S BEHAVIOR

WORKBOOK

CONTENTS

STUDY 1 7
Chapter 1: Why Your Kids Do What They Do
Chapter 2: The Five Emotional Gauges of a Teenager

STUDY 2 15
Chapter 3: When Needs Are Met
Chapter 4: When Needs Aren't Met
Chapter 5: Teens and Relationships

STUDY 3 21
Chapter 6: Looking in the Mirror
Chapter 7: Looking at the Past
Chapter 8: Looking to the Future

STUDY 4 27
Chapter 9: Actions and Attitudes that Speak Louder than Words
Chapter 12: Relationship Goals

STUDY 5 33
Chapter 10: Listening to Your Teen
Chapter 11: Healing the Hurts
Chapter 13: Conclusion
Read James 1:19, Ephesians 4:2, Ephesians 4:32

STUDY 1

RELATED CHAPTERS

Chapter 1: Why Your Kids Do What They Do

Chapter 2: The Five Emotional Gauges of a Teenager

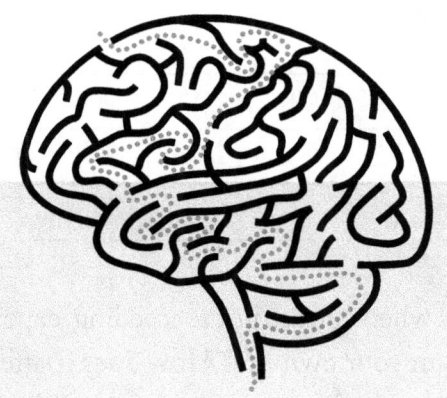

OBJECTIVE

To explore the link between needs and behavior and to evaluate the five emotional gauges and their related needs.

1.

What motivates you as an adult to get out of bed every morning, go to work, attend meetings, check email, scroll through social media, attend church, workout, connect with friends?

_____

_____

_____

_____

To what extent do spiritual, financial, physical, emotional, and relational needs play in your own life?

_____

_____

_____

_____

How do you feel when you are not succeeding, experience setbacks or deal with stress in your own life? How does it affect the way you think, feel, and your attitude and actions in your life?

_____

_____

_____

_____

The same is true for teenagers. Needs drive teenagers' behavior when it comes to what they believe, how they think, feel, and what they do.

REVIEW THE STATISTICS ON PAGE 20 IN CHAPTER 1.

These statistics reveal real issues and struggles teenagers are facing in their lives. When you peel back the layers of each teenager's life, you can almost always find that the root problem behind their negative thinking, emotions, attitudes, and behaviors are often a result of unmet spiritual, emotional, and relational needs—specifically real needs that are often overlooked or go unmet at home. When a teenager's needs are met by healthy relationships with parents and other caring adults, a teenager will be more likely to have positive self-esteem, attitudes, and positive behavior. When needs are unmet by busy, distracted or disengaged parents, teenagers may look to social media or seek relationships with those whose values are negative, immoral, and even destructive, as long as those people offer acceptance, approval, and attention.

READ GENESIS 2:18

When God created the heavens and the earth, God placed Adam in a perfect world, yet God still said, "It is not good." Adam was sinless, innocent in heart and mind. He had everything he needed in the garden, he even had an exalted position. He was put in charge over everything. Even though Adam enjoyed an intimate relationship with God, God still said, "It is not good for man to be alone." With all the spiritual, and physical needs in his life being met, God created Adam with a need for human relationships. Even though God was all Adam needed to be the primary supplier of his needs, God still wanted to bless Adam with human relationships where he could experience the joy of giving and receiving from others to meet his relational needs.

How much do you look to or depend upon others for acceptance, approval, attention, love, support, encouragement, etc?

_____
_____
_____
_____

Would you agree that your teenager is driven by those same needs?

_____
_____
_____
_____

2.

Teenagers' needs are intensified by the rapid developmental changes that occur during this needy time.

••

READ "AND YOU THOUGHT YOU HAD NEEDS" IN CHAPTER 2.

••

Make a list of *emotions* you see in teenagers that are associated with each developmental area. Then make a list of *needs* you see in teenagers that are associated with the developmental process. For example, under physical development, the emotions list might include embarrassment, confusion, frustration; the needs list might be acceptance of your teenager's lack of coordination, reassurance that pains in body are normal, support that they are growing up.

3.

Define authentic needs using the information on page 37 in chapter 2.

••

READ 2 CORINTHIANS 1:4.

••

God comforts us in our needs so we can comfort others. Read Philippians 4:19. God is the supplier of all our needs.

4.

••

REVIEW THE NEEDS ACROSTIC (CHAPTER 2) AND THE FIVE BASIC GAUGES.

••

These emotional gauges are similar to the gauges in a car, monitoring what is operating correctly and what isn't.

What are some ways teenagers seek attention?

_____
_____
_____
_____

How can a parent tell when the need for attention in a teenager is low?

_____

_____

_____

5.

Consider asking your teen to fill out the Needs Evaluation at the end of chapter 2.

• •

CLOSE WITH A PRAYER THANKING GOD FOR THE GIFT OF YOUR TEENAGER.

• •

NOTES

NOTES

STUDY 2

RELATED CHAPTERS

Chapter 3: When Needs Are Met

Chapter 4: When Needs Aren't Met

Chapter 5: Teens and Relationships

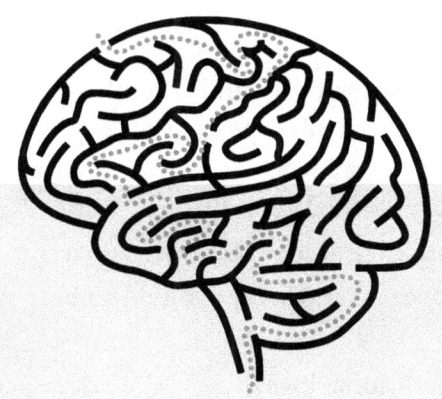

OBJECTIVE

To recognize the difference between met and unmet needs; to help determine your teenager's primary need; to see how a close relationship helps parents determine and meet those critical needs.

PROCEDURE

1.

Check each statement that is true for you:
- ❏ I have never been angry.
- ❏ My home is always neat and clean.
- ❏ I never raise my voice.
- ❏ I compliment my spouse daily.
- ❏ I speak politely to everyone in my family at all times.
- ❏ I smile all day long.
- ❏ I always remember to do my chores at home with a pleasant attitude.
- ❏ I support family members in everything they do.
- ❏ I never criticize a family member.
- ❏ I never have embarrassed a family member.
- ❏ I am successful at work 100 percent of the time.

Did you meet any of those conditions? Notice how those statements could be conditional love statements parents make to teens. For example, "I'll love you and accept you if you keep your room clean all the time."

» What is unconditional love?
» How can we show unconditional love to our teenagers?
» Why is it so hard to love unconditionally?
» How does unconditional love relate to needs?

• •

REREAD THE UNCONDITIONAL LOVE MATCH-UP UNDER "GIVE UNCONDITIONAL LOVE" ON PAGE 175 IN CHAPTER 8.

• •

2.

REREAD "A PARENTAL INVESTIGATOR" IN CHAPTER 3.

Review each of the three scenarios and responses, and complete the statements following the scenarios.

Needs drive the thoughts and feelings that lead to behavior. Turn to the Emotional Gauge chart under "How Emotional Gauges Work" on page 78 in chapter 3. Notice how each gauge results in constructive thinking, favorable feelings, and appropriate behaviors when needs are met in healthy situations. Now compare that to the Emotional Gauge chart under "Unmasking the Needs" on page 88 in chapter 4 to see how the gauges change when there are unmet needs, or needs met by negative sources. Follow the thinking, feeling, and behaving pattern of each gauge. When needs go unmet, teenagers often assume a mask to hide their thoughts, feelings, and behavior. Remember this quote from Walt Mueller, "If we choose not to mold and shape our children, someone else will." How does that statement relate to the thinking, feeling, behaving emotional gauge charts? Review the masks discussed in chapter 4 during the coming week. Also review the roles parents may assume to hide for their inability or unwillingness to meet their teenager's needs.

3.

If needs drive behavior, relationships form the means through which emotional needs are met. The deeper, more secure the relationship between a parent and teen, the greater the possibility that the need will be met and the teenager will function in a healthy way. The less connected, superficial relationships may result in an unmet need.

••

REVIEW THE "SUPERFICIAL RELATIONSHIP, AUTHENTIC RELATIONSHIP" LISTING UNDER "RELATIONSHIP CONNECTIONS" ON PAGE 106 IN CHAPTER 5.

••

Circle the words that best describe your relationship with your teenager. If you have circled more words under "Superficial Relationship" than under "Authentic Relationship," then perhaps you need to find ways to develop the relationship into a deeper, more connected relationship. Reread the discussion of four skills that can help a family improve its relationships: the skills of caring, trusting, giving, and loving. How can you improve the skill of caring? trusting? giving? loving?

4.

Parents intentionally or unintentionally can be their own worst enemy in building and maintaining relationships. Make a list of "Do's" and "Don't's" for building positive relationships with your teen. Select your top three in each list. If you need help getting started, review the "Relationship Blunders" and "Relationship Building" sections in chapter 5.

••

READ I JOHN 3:18.

••

NOTES

NOTES

STUDY 3

RELATED CHAPTERS

Chapter 6: Looking in the Mirror

Chapter 7: Looking at the Past

Chapter 8: Looking to the Future

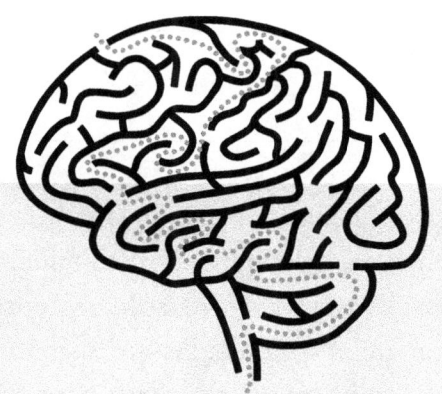

OBJECTIVE

To evaluate the unmet needs during your teenage years, to face painful memories, and to get your needs met today in a healthy manner.

READ PHILIPPIANS 1:6, PHILIPPIANS 2:13, AND PHILIPPIANS 3:13.

PROCEDURE:

1.

Complete the statement: "When I grow up and become a parent, I'll never …"

_____

_____

_____

Parenting is a learned behavior based on what you saw modeled at home. Unless you make a deliberate effort to understand your past and change your reactions, you will most likely repeat the behavior modeled by your parents. If you had healthy parenting role models, you learned healthy parenting practices. But none of us had perfect parents, so along the way we learned imperfect parenting behavior.

REREAD "LOOK IN THE MIRROR AND DISCOVER" ON PAGE 135 IN CHAPTER 6.

Parents cannot effectively meet a teenager's needs without first having needs met in their lives.

2.

When you were a teenager, what were your favorite family events, traditions, celebrations, or rituals?

_____
_____
_____

Most of the time how did you feel about these?

_____
_____
_____

Which of these ceremonies or traditions have you carried over into your present-day family? Why?

_____
_____
_____

• •

TURN TO "WHEN I WAS A TEENAGER..." ON PAGE 138 IN CHAPTER 6.

• •

List two or three behaviors that were negative, inappropriate, even destructive, or two or three positive behaviors. With your spouse or a friend, share one or two of these behaviors (positives or negatives). Discuss what needs went unmet based on the negative behavior, or which needs were met based on the positive behavior. This exercise is not about blaming, but about understanding how your past behavior was driven by your own needs.

There is no magic formula to bring healing to your past. But there are several steps suggested in chapter 7 that can help the healing begin.

••

REVIEW THE SIX STEPS UNDER "LET THE HEALING BEGIN" ON PAGE 155 AND COMPLETE THE DIFFERENT REFLECTIVE ACTIVITIES TO EVALUATE YOUR PAST.

••

3.

Now it's time to turn to the present. Since God made everyone with needs, then adults have needs too. Complete the needs information on pages 144 and 145 at the end of chapter 6, using a scale of one to ten. Keep these needs in mind as you study this material. Parents can also get into inappropriate, unhealthy behavior by looking toward the wrong people to meet their needs. Who are the healthy types of people who can meet your needs today? How can these people know what needs you have and how to meet them? Teenagers cannot fully meet the needs of their parents, except indirectly as the parent experiences joy over seeing their teenager mature.

Draw a family crest that expresses what your family values today. Your crest may include a symbol or word for each family member, a symbol or word for a special, annual family event, a symbol or word for a strength you see in your family, a symbol or word for a weakness or a missing ingredient, a symbol or word for the relationships in the family.

4.

REVIEW THE ABCs FOR MAINTAINING A BALANCE AS PARENTS MEET THEIR TEENAGER'S NEEDS.

These are under "ABCs for the Future" on page 169 in chapter 8. Offer a prayer to God, praying for:
- your past, including people in your past and events that were positive and negative;
- your present, mentioning the needs you have in your life and the desire to find the appropriate person to help meet those needs;
- your future with your teenager and other family members, that change might happen if it is needed and allow the healing to begin.

NOTES

STUDY 4

RELATED CHAPTERS

Chapter 9: Actions and Attitudes that Speak Louder than Words

Chapter 12: Relationship Goals

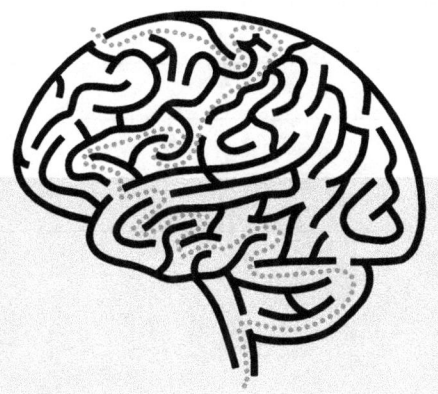

OBJECTIVE

To identify specific actions you can take to meet your teenager's needs, how meeting these needs can change behavior, and how to set goals that encourage change

1.

It's 1 a.m. You realize your seventeen-year-old teenager is not home yet. You check your son's location on your phone, and realize he is not where he said he was going. You try calling and texting him but he is not responding. Suddenly, you hear the key turn in the outside door, and your teenager is standing before you asking, "What are you doing up?" You respond . . . Would your actions and attitude have been different before studying this book? How might your actions and attitude change? Turn to chapter 9 and read the two lists that describe parents. Point out the comparison listing at the beginning of chapter 9. What in this revolutionary relationship approach of meeting the teenager's needs have you found most helpful?

_____
_____
_____
_____

2.

Think about the conflicts and struggles you have with your teenagers (allowance, curfew, language, homework, getting a job, doing the chores around the house, etc.) Is this a conflict caused by the teenager's emotional development or an unmet need? How can you tell which needs are involved in different conflicts?

_____
_____
_____
_____

3.

NOTICE THE FIVE GAUGES WITH THE RELATED NEEDS THAT MAKE UP CHAPTER 9.

Review the ideas under each need and think of two or three of the actions that might be effective in meeting that need. Have you been able to determine your teenager's primary need at this time? Which ideas have you read that you think will be useable? Which ideas or actions can you put into action immediately?

_____
_____
_____
_____

Parenting is not an exact science, therefore, the trial-and-error method sometimes has to be used.

4.

You are now at the place where you can begin to make some changes in your relationships with your teenagers and set goals for changing other behavior.

REVIEW THE INFORMATION ABOUT GOALS UNDER "HOW TO SET A GOAL" ON PAGE 255 IN CHAPTER 12.

Look at the first set of goals under "My Personal Goals" on page 258 in chapter 12. Write a goal for yourself with a simple plan and a possible date. Working with your spouse, set one of the "Goals Involving the Family" on page 259 in chapter 12. Finally, set one of the "Goals Involving My Teenager" on page 260 in chapter 12. Goals can either be "wish lists" with little meaning because little effort has been applied or life-changing plans that are carried out with planning, desire, and work.

5.

How did you respond to the opening scenario of being out past curfew at 1 A.M.?

• •

READ THE CLOSING TWO PARAGRAPHS FROM CHAPTER 9.

• •

What do you think would happen from that point on?

Close your eyes and picture yourself standing in the doorway as your teenager(s) opens the door. How would you start the conversation? How would you end the conversation? What would be the best and most productive way to understand his side of the story while remaining firm on your expectations? How could you respond to the situation affirming your deep love and concern without compromising your expectations for curfew? How could you turn that situation into a growth opportunity?

_____
_____
_____
_____

NOTES

NOTES

STUDY 5

RELATED CHAPTERS

Chapter 10: Listening to Your Teen

Chapter 11: Healing the Hurts

Chapter 13: Conclusion

Read James 1:19, Ephesians 4:2, Ephesians 4:32

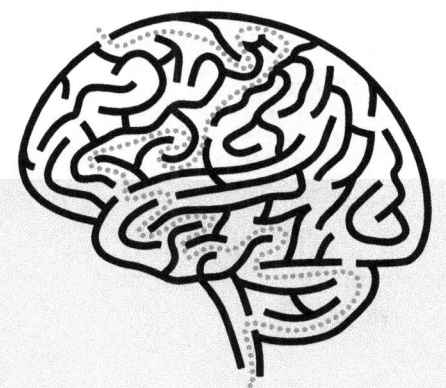

OBJECTIVE

To learn how to improve communication with your teenagers, deal with conflict, and handle the deepest hurts

PROCEDURE:

1.

Make a "Top Ten List" of the things parents would like to hear from their teenagers.

••

READ THE "TOP TEN" LIST AT THE BEGINNING OF CHAPTER 13.

••

While teenagers might not say these particular things, they do say something. Part of building a relationship and meeting your teenager's needs requires communication.

2.

What frustrations do you have in communicating with your teenager? How do we as parents block communication or make it difficult for our teens to talk with us?

_____
_____
_____
_____

••

REVIEW THE SIX COMMUNICATION BLOCKERS UNDER "SIX COMMUNICATION BLOCKERS" ON PAGE 205 IN CHAPTER 10.

••

What other attitudes or actions block communication? How can you overcome these frustrating blockers and create more positive communication?

_____

_____

_____

_____

LOOK AT THE "NINE WAYS TO LISTEN TO TEENAGERS" ON PAGE 208 IN CHAPTER 10.

Think of examples of each.

One of the frustrations of teenagers is always hearing the word "no." In the coming week, make a mental note to see how frequently you say "no." Think about ways you can say "yes" instead.

3.

Even in the most loving families, conflict arises.
- How do you handle conflicts in your family?
- How can you defuse an angry teenager?
- What makes you the angriest?
- How can you resolve the conflict without having a winner and a loser?
- Do all conflicts need to be resolved?
- What happens if conflicts go unaddressed?

•••

REVIEW "A FIVE-STEP PROCESS TO REDUCE AND RESOLVE CONFLICT" ON PAGE 215 IN CHAPTER 10.

•••

One of your conflicts may be over past hurt that has not healed. This kind of hurt results in open wounds that can't be corrected by reestablishing a relationship. Chapter 11 deals with "Healing the Hurts."

4.

In looking to the future, ask yourself these questions:
- What are some of your greatest fears for your teenager?
- What are some of your greatest hopes for your teenager?
- Which do you think will win out with your teenager— the fears or the hopes? Why?

As parents, you are doing better than you think you are, and you matter more to your teenager than you think you do. Remember, life is long, stay encouraged. Life is short, live intentional. You got this!

NOTES

NOTES

NOTES

NOTES

NOTES

NOTES

www.ingramcontent.com/pod-product-compliance
Lightning Source LLC
Chambersburg PA
CBHW070654100426
42734CB00048B/2987